Praise for actual air

"David Berman possesses the most engrossing new poetic voice I have heard in many years of hard listening. When I first read him, I thought: so this is the voice I have been waiting so long to hear, a voice, I wish in some poems, were my own. Any reader who tunes into his snappy, off-beat meditations is in for a steady infusion of surprises and delights."   —*Billy Collins*

"*Actual Air* is one of the funniest, smartest, and sweetest books of the year, a collection of snapshots colored ecstatically outside the lines. This is the absurd American sublime, poetry that raises the stakes on the everyday and bluffs the bluffers."   —*GQ*

"When was the last time you picked up a volume of poetry and found yourself hanging on every word, reading it all the way through in a single sitting and then going back to the beginning? This first collection from Berman is that kind of book. Full of casually sharp observations about the most mundane subjects. *Air* is funny, weird, and profound, whether it's tackling the nature of hallways or the architecture of back pain."   —*Entertainment Weekly*

"In Berman's universe, time slips lazily on by, life is thoroughly strange and perpetually interesting, and there's no reason why a man shouldn't sit down on a Thursday afternoon in May and learn some new facts about animals."   —*Time Out New York*

"*Actual Air* is actual poetry. Berman is on a mission to make the world strange, to find in the doo-dads of daily life a profound weirdness...which makes for a rarity in contemporary poetry."   —*Spin*

"Berman's debut announces the discovery of a great American poetic storytelling voice by a new generation."
                                                      —*Publishers Weekly*

actual air

Poems by David Berman

 **OPEN CITY BOOKS**

OPEN CITY BOOKS

270 Lafayette Street, Suite 1412
New York, NY 10012
www.opencity.org

Designed by Meghan Gerety

Cover photograph by Roe Ethridge
Author photograph by Bernd Bodtländer

Manufactured in the United States of America

12   11   10   9   8

Eighth Printing, 2008

Library of Congress Catalog Card Number: 99-63712

These poems have previously appeared in the following publications:
"Cantos for James Michener: Part II," "Democratic Vistas," "Community
College in the Rain," and "Nervous Ashers" in *The Baffler*; "Self-Portrait
at 28" and "Cassette County" in *Purple*; "Tableau Through Shattered
Monacle" in the *Coe Review*; "Governors on Sominex," "If There Was a Book
About This Hallway," "Classic Water," "Serenade for a Wealthy Widow,"
"Now II," and "A Letter from Isaac Asimov to His Wife Janet, Written On His
Deathbed" in *Open City*.

ISBN-10: 1-890447-04-8
ISBN-13: 978-1-890447-04-5

to
MICHELE

CONTENTS

1.

2.

3.

1.

Snow

Walking through a field with my little brother Seth

I pointed to a place where kids had made angels in the snow.
For some reason, I told him that a troop of angels
had been shot and dissolved when they hit the ground.

He asked who had shot them and I said a farmer.

Then we were on the roof of the lake.
The ice looked like a photograph of water.

Why he asked. Why did he shoot them.

I didn't know where I was going with this.

They were on his property, I said.

When it's snowing, the outdoors seem like a room.

Today I traded hellos with my neighbor.
Our voices hung close in the new acoustics.
A room with the walls blasted to shreds and falling.

We returned to our shoveling, working side by side in silence.

But why were they on his property, he asked.

Classic Water

I remember Kitty saying we shared a deep longing for
the consolation prize, laughing as we rinsed the stagecoach.

I remember the night we camped out
            and I heard her whisper
"think of me as a place" from her sleeping bag
            with the centaur print.

I remember being in her father's basement workshop
when we picked up an unknown man sobbing
over the shortwave radio

and the night we got so high we convinced ourselves
that the road was a hologram projected by the headlight beams.

I remember how she would always get everyone to vote
on what we should do next and the time she said
"all water is classic water" and shyly turned her face away.

At volleyball games her parents sat in the bleachers
like ambassadors from Indiana in all their midwestern schmaltz.

She was destroyed when they were busted for operating
a private judicial system within U.S. borders.

Sometimes I'm awakened in the middle of the night
by the clatter of a room service cart and I think back on Kitty.

Those summer evenings by the government lake,
talking about the paradox of multiple Santas
or how it felt to have your heart broken.

I still get a hollow feeling on Labor Day when the summer ends

and I remember how I would always refer to her boyfriends
as what's-his-face, which was wrong of me and I'd like
to apologize to those guys right now, wherever they are:

No one deserves to be called what's-his-face.

Civics

She had been the court stenographer
in the little village for two decades
when she disappeared into the mountains.

I was part of the search party that day.
Snow was pending and the bare branches
looked like mounted antlers on the canyon walls.

I walked with Glenn from White Moon Insurance
for hours through columns of shimmering firs
and over ponds frozen into opal tables

until, arriving at an overlook at dusk,
we heard the cracking of a hammer
echoing through the burnished valley
and saw what looked like the old judge
and twelve other men and women
pitching camp for the night.

Governors on Sominex

It had been four days of no weather
as if nature had conceded its genius to the indoors.

They'd closed down the Bureau of Sad Endings
and my wife sat on the couch and read the paper out loud.

The evening edition carried the magic death of a child
backlit by a construction site sunrise on its front page.

I kept my back to her and fingered the items on the mantle.

Souvenirs only reminded you of buying them.

The moon hung solid over the boarded-up Hobby Shop.

P.K. was in the precinct house, using his one phone call
to dedicate a song to Tammy, for she was the light
by which he traveled into this and that.

And out in the city, out in the wide readership,
his younger brother was kicking an ice bucket
in the woods behind the Marriott,

his younger brother who was missing that part of the brain
that allows you to make out with your pillow.

Poor kid.

It was the light in things that made them last.

* * *

Tammy called her caseworker from a closed gas station
to relay ideas unaligned with the world we loved.

The tall grass bent in the wind like tachometer needles
and he told her to hang in there, slowly repeating
the number of the Job Info Line.

She hung up and glared at the Killbuck Sweet Shoppe.
The words that had been running through her head,
"employees must wash hands before returning to work,"
kept repeating and the sky looked dead.

* * *

Hedges formed the long limousine a Tampa sky could die behind.
A sailor stood on the wharf with a clipper ship
reflected on the skin of the bell pepper he held.

He'd had mouthwash at the inn and could still feel
the ice blue carbon pinwheels spinning in his mouth.

There were no new ways to understand the world,
only new days to set our understandings against.

Through the lanes came virgins in tennis shoes,
their hair shining like videotape,

singing us into a kind of sleep we hadn't tried yet.

Each page was a new chance to understand the last.

And somehow the sea was always there to make you feel stupid.

The Spine of the Snowman

On the moon, an old caretaker in faded clothes is holed up in his
pressurized cabin. The fireplace is crackling, casting sparks onto the
instrument panel. His eyes are flickering over the earth,

looking for Illinois,

looking for his hometown, Gnarled Heritage,
    until his sight is caught in its chimneys and frosted aerials.

He thinks back on the jeweler's son who skated the pond
behind his house, and the local supermarket with aisles
that curved off like country roads.

Yesterday the robot had been asking him about snowmen.
He asked if they had minds.
No, the caretaker said, but he'd seen one
that had a raccoon burrowed up inside the head.

"Most had a carrot nose, some coal, buttons, and twigs for arms,
but others were more complex.
Once they started to melt, things would rise up
from inside the body. Maybe a gourd, which was an organ,
or a long knobbed stick, which was the spine of the snowman."

The robot shifted uncomfortably in his chair.

The Coahoma County Wind Cults

My dream walked on four legs
toward the remote source
of a pale yellow letter

only to circle around the cabin
when it got there.

A black and white cave rainbow
arched between two old shoes.

Oxygen bounced off the face of a doll,
looking for the slow dazzling guts
of a life form.

There was a moment of sudden clarity
when the pages burned in opera glasses,

like a herd crossing zip codes

or an exhumed idea pressing
at the limits of the marquee bulbs,

my dream pushes air.

Imagining Defeat

She woke me up at dawn,
her suitcase like a little brown dog at her heels.

I sat up and looked out the window
at the snow falling in the stand of blackjack trees.

A bus ticket in her hand.

Then she brought something black up to her mouth,
a plum I thought, but it was an asthma inhaler.

I reached under the bed for my menthols
and she asked if I ever thought of cancer.

Yes, I said, but always as a tree way up ahead
in the distance where it doesn't matter.

And I suppose a dead soul must look back at that tree,
so far behind his wagon where it also doesn't matter

except as a memory of rest or water.

Though to believe any of that, I thought,
you have to accept the premise

that she woke me up at all.

Tableau Through Shattered Monocle

His house had white brick balconies, chiseled drapes,
and starcharts beneath the wallpaper. There was the smell of English
plastic, and a mud racetrack out back where a smacked up car with
garlands of nicks in the paint waited lamely in the paddock.

We found a burnt keyboard by the millrace, blackbirds stacked
in the cabinets, and heard how the house made little cracking
sounds when he got up in the morning to wade through pages
of labyrinthine Spanish logic or dismantle chunks of mica.

The professor said that a herald on a dirtbike broke up the driveway
bearing hill testimony from a cult called The People, and that something
felt wrong when he heard a boat hiss below the planks
and the man say "if my John Adams hand shoots."

Sometimes driveways develop endzones so more imaginary Swedens
can rise from the bottom of the book, but in our historical reassessment
of the Redcoats we forget the peace in a name like James
or the long rainy Indian wars, fought primarily in the nude.

The squad feels new in new rooms and our attention
sometimes clots on a detail, like this scotch tape, clear as a highland
stream, repairing file folders entitled "How car keys think"
and "Not a still life but a slow life then."

During investigations the void may bloom in the mirror like twin
wedding dresses on a high thin bed, but these apparitions
are not evidence, they're not even sediment. It's all slush at the
foxes' feet, a frieze of braille, photos of the isotopes.

We'd had hot and cold conversations in dead languages for years,
yet the installation and plugging in of moons, the slight changes in
the rules of tennis, the thought that "we could be losing" never
completely crossed our minds.

Perhaps it took the marriage of Now and Then, here in the weeks
leading up to football season, to make us realize that in death we are
declassified, whether it arrives in European forests that smell like attics
or while negotiating a curve by the college library—

these words are meant to mark this day on earth.

If There Was a Book About This Hallway

It would start, There is a road within the home

some pine slats in the corner

and lamps along the walls that give the path an endlessness
at night.

I remember the day I left the meterman standing in the hall.

In my room I drew his hard apple face as he waited
in the cold shade.

No matter how slight, it is a scene from history.
A scene from the book.

Are dreams set in hallways because the perspective is screwed?

Or because they are the long, open, unused stages in our homes?

The hallway was a dry riverbed I dreamed one night,

                    an Indian turnpike on another.

(And it may have been those things before the house was here.)

I never heard the meterman leave but saw he was gone

when I went out to hang his sketch on the wall.

Sour furniture-polish winds rolled down the dark corridor.

Once a fir where each door now stands.

If Christ had died in a hallway we might pray in hallways
or wear little golden hallways around our necks.

How can it still be unwarmed after so many passings?

An outdoors that is somehow indoors.

Narrated by a Committee

The enameled moon
rode over the long cool world
as we stepped outside to get some air.

Birds from other area codes
sang their Precambrian songs,

the light pulse of the seminary
faded in the wax trees,

and we, the committee, strolled around
talking about the burden of inheritance tax
and the elegance of watering cans.

We walked between Hill 49 and Hill 50,
then over the old river,
which was slow and thin for miles,
before it disappeared underground.

At the park's wild core,
where lamp posts frontier the old dark,
we saw fountains remaking themselves
over and over again,

we saw the night leaking out the western doors
and discussed returning to the committee room,
to the oak chairs, ice water and gavels

when the sound of snapping branches
made us turn to see
the caribou crossing the Nikon.

Cassette County

This is meant to be in praise of the interval called hangover,
a sadness not co-terminous with hopelessness,
and the North American doubling cascade
that (keep going) "this diamond lake is a photo lab"
and if predicates really do propel the plot
then you might see Jerusalem in a soap bubble
or the appliance failures on Olive Street
across these great instances,
because "the complex Italians versus the basic Italians"
because what does a mirror look like (when it's not working)
but birds singing a full tone higher in the sunshine.

I'm going to call them Honest Eyes until I know if they are,
in the interval called *slam-clicker*, Realm of Pacific,
because the second language wouldn't let me learn it
because I have heard of you for a long time occasionally
because diet cards may be the recovery evergreen
and there is a new benzodiazepene called Distance,

anti-showmanship, anti-showmanship, anti-showmanship.

I suppose a broken window is not symbolic
unless symbolic means broken, which I think it sorta does,
and when the phone jangles
what's more radical, the snow or the tires,
and what does the Bible say about metal fatigue
and why do mothers carry big scratched-up sunglasses
in their purses.

Hello to the era of going to the store to buy more ice
because we are running out.
Hello to feelings that arrive unintroduced.
Hello to the nonfunctional sprig of parsley
and the game of finding meaning in coincidence.

Because there is a second mind in the margins of the used book
because Judas Priest (source: Firestone Library)
sang a song called Stained Class,
because this world is 66% Then and 33% Now,

and if you wake up thinking "feeling is a skill now"
or "even this glass of water seems complicated now"
and a phrase from a men's magazine (like single-district cognac)
rings and rings in your neck,
then let the consequent misunderstandings
(let the changer love the changed)
wobble on heartbreakingly nu legs
into this street-legal nonfiction,
into this good world,
this warm place
that I love with all my heart,

anti-showmanship, anti-showmanship, anti-showmanship.

World: Series

When something passes in the dark
I make a note on a pad kept by the window.

Candlelight wobbles on the walls,
over the baseboard electrical outlets
that look like primitive swine masks

and I can't remember if I read or dreamed about them—
a sect on the Mayflower called the Strangers—
four or five adults who gathered in the hold
and spoke to no one through the three month passage.

When the boats landed on the beach
they walked into the North American forest
and were never seen again.

I put my book down and come to the window
where curtains are fastened to the sides
so it is like looking out at the world
through the back of a teenage girl's head

and my signature is drawn in magic marker
on the lower right hand corner of the window

so when something passes in the dark
it's captured for a moment inside my work.

I come to the window and title the eras
Monday, Tuesday, Wednesday,

and watch the wind in the tension of the blown trees,
the moon illuminated by my attention.
When something passes in the dark,
I try to tell its side of the story.

"I am passing someone in the dark," it thinks...

Tulsa

A woman named Tina drinks gin at sunset
before a pair of drawn curtains that frame
the dry grasslands and tangerine hilltops
of her native county. An insurance bill
is pinned to the desk top by a calculator.
The curtains are purple.

The man she intends to marry is reserved
as a dark prairie pond. He paints radio storms
in the basement beside a globe of Mars,
his hair and shoes the color of ox blood.

The local graveyard is now run
by the management company he owns.
Stones are strewn on the even pathways
like the exploded bits of a larger rock.
Annually, starlings fill the trees
as if commanded by a book on Death.

And she, a manicurist who digs the intimacy
of her work, holds hands for a living.
Perfecting the extremities of oilmen and bankers.

But this man, this man she intends to marry,
is strange. She wonders, What's the deal with
quiet people, can they read minds? Just then

a junebug flies in and lands on a curtain.
The purple curtain on her right.
My left, her right.

Community College in the Rain

Announcement: All pupils named Doug.
Please come to the lounge on Concourse K.

Please join us for coffee and remarks.

Dougs: We cannot come. We are injured by golf cleats.

Announcement: Today we will discuss the energy in a wing
and something about first basemen.

Ribs will be served in the cafeteria.

Pep Club: We will rally against golf cleats today.
The rally will be held behind the gymnasium.

There is a Model T in the parking lot with its lights on.

Dougs: We are dying in the nurse's office.
When she passes before the window, she looks like a bride.

Karen (whispers): We are ranking the great shipwrecks.

Announcement: In the classroom filled with dishwater light,

Share your thoughts on public sculpture.

All: O Dougs, where are you?

Dougs: In the wild hotels of the sea.

The Charm of 5:30

It's too nice a day to read a novel set in England.

We're within inches of the perfect distance from the sun,
the sky is blueberries and cream,
and the wind is as warm as air from a tire.
Even the headstones in the graveyard
          seem to stand up and say "Hello! My name is..."

It's enough to be sitting here on my porch,
thinking about Kermit Roosevelt,
following the course of an ant,
or walking out into the yard with a cordless phone
          to find out she is going to be there tonight.

On a day like today, what looks like bad news in the distance
turns out to be something on my contact, carports and white
courtesy phones are spontaneously reappreciated
          and random "okay"s ring through the backyards.

This morning I discovered the red tints in cola
          when I held a glass of it up to the light
and found an expensive flashlight in the pocket of a winter coat
          I was packing away for summer.

It all reminds me of that moment when you take off your sunglasses
after a long drive and realize it's earlier
and lighter out than you had accounted for.

You know what I'm talking about,

and that's the kind of fellowship that's taking place in town, out in
the public spaces. You won't overhear anyone using the words
"dramaturgy" or "state inspection" today. We're too busy getting along.

It occurs to me that the laws are in the regions and the regions are in the laws, and it feels good to say this, something that I'm almost sure is true, outside under the sun.

Then to say it again, around friends, in the resonant voice of a nineteenth-century senator, just for a lark.

There's a shy looking fellow on the courthouse steps, holding up a placard that says "But, I kinda liked Reagan." His head turns slowly as a beautiful girl walks by, holding a refrigerated bottle up against her flushed cheek.

She smiles at me and I allow myself to imagine her walking into town to buy lotion at a brick pharmacy.
When she gets home she'll apply it with great lingering care before moving into her parlor to play 78 records and drink gin-and-tonics beside her homemade altar to James Madison.

In a town of this size, it's certainly possible that I'll be invited over one night.

In fact I'll bet you something.

Somewhere in the future I am remembering today. I'll bet you
I'm remembering how I walked into the park at five thirty,
my favorite time of day, and how I found two cold pitchers
of just poured beer, sitting there on the bench.

I am remembering how my friend Chip showed up
with a catcher's mask hanging from his belt and how I said

great to see you, sit down, have a beer, how are you,
and how he turned to me with the sunset reflecting off his contacts
and said, wonderful, how are you.

The Moon

A web of sewer, pipe, and wire connects each house to the others.

In 206 a dog sleeps by the stove where a small gas leak causes him
to have visions; visions that are rooted in nothing but gas.

Next door, a man who has decided to buy a car part by part
excitedly unpacks a wheel and an ashtray.

He arranges them every which way. It's really beginning to take
shape.

Out the garage window he sees a group of ugly children
enter the forest. Their mouths look like coin slots.

A neighbor plays keyboards in a local cover band.
Preparing for an engagement at the high school prom,

they pack their equipment in silence.

Last night they played the Police Academy Ball and all
the officers slow-danced with target range silhouettes.

This year the theme for the prom is the Tetragrammaton.

A yellow Corsair sails through the disco parking lot
and swaying palms presage the lot of young libertines.

Inside the car a young lady wears a corsage of bullet-sized rodents.
Her date, the handsome cornerback, stretches his talons over the
molded steering wheel.

They park and walk into the lush starlit gardens behind the disco just as the band is striking up.

Their keen eyes and ears twitch. The other couples
look beautiful tonight. They stroll around listening
to the brilliant conversation. The passionate speeches.

Clouds drift across the silverware. There is red larkspur,
blue gum, and ivy. A boy kneels before his date.

And the moon, I forgot to mention the moon.

2.

From Cantos for James Michener: Part II

CI.

The jets move slowly through the sky like they'll never
reach Denver or wherever they're going,

and I have the feeling that people are high-fiving nearby,

spontaneously, like a saloon brawl where everyone
suddenly starts fighting as if each man has
a preconscious knowledge of which side he's on
when he enters a crowded room.

And this fight starts with a Polish joke that a man
at the bar begins to tell, but it's not funny
as it concerns a stillborn child and an alcoholic
slain by the last European wolf, and even after
three hours there is no punchline in sight.

When he reaches the part where a Polish scientist
who has been navigating through millimeters of wilderness
discovers sub-atomic temples in a rust sample,
none of the men are listening,

they are thinking about their own childhoods

about the deep embarrassment of scoring on your own team

and the view from falling behind.

CXI.

(If you have ever quit an imaginary job over an imaginary paycut,

mistakenly taken your house's thermostat for a dial
with which to focus the windows,

written a play about the special relationship that blooms
when a withdrawn honor student is assigned to tutor
the school's basketball star,

fallen in love with the woman who plays the part
of your character's wife and bears you a child
that can communicate with rust,

been deafened by the panoply of voices in the classifieds

tied up every private detective in town with false leads,

taken photos of people saying "shut up,"

or know a place where you can get married at midnight,

then you know what I'm talking about.)

CIX.

The Smokers were encamped on a rivulet in the south forty.
Their leader, a tall housewife decorated with medals from
the Virginia and North Carolina state legislatures,
sucked on a menthol 100 and scanned the cured fields.

I whistled when I got within earshot to let them know
I was coming. The Smoker children ran out to meet me
and I passed out nicotine gum and colorful matchbooks.

I lit up and approached the oak tree where the leader's
tent was pitched. She stared at me contemptuously and
opened her bathrobe. I sucked on each breast for a second.
She motioned for me to sit on the beer chest.

It was my land they were camping on but it sure didn't
feel like it. She stuck a cigarette in her mouth and I
jumped up to light it.

"Sit down," she said. "Did you bring the scratch tickets?"
"Here they are."
"What are they saying in town?"
"There are rumors of a sale."

XCVI.

He wasn't sure how the bathroom mirror worked
but decided it must be powered
by the razor blades and aspirin
he found in the engine compartment.

It was a matter of relearning everything
after he surfaced from the coma.

The hospital chapel had bought a battered
fog machine from a local heavy metal band
that broke up over disagreements about
Viking iconography.

Sitting in the back row, he began to pray
for his hospital roommate, suffering
under the byzantine complexity of back pain.

He said it felt like he was laying
on top of an architect's model of a small town
whose five-story bank building commanded
a view of the plains.

Clouds of steam drifted around his ankles.

CII.

The waiting room across the hall
was filled with hostile stepsons.

He was studying their faces when his favorite nurse
came in to show him an x-ray of a scarecrow
she had found in the chapel.

Someone had written "the unborn God
of the $C_8H_{17}NO_4S$ Indians" on the bottom.

"Here, this pill should make you feel like a turtle
tangled up in a dry cleaning bag."

The nurses are so beautiful, he thought.
Try to remember that they are covered in germs.

CV.

He woke up at 12:34 and saw the Mirrornauts
standing by the full-length mirror in their chrome uniforms.

Their scouts had already crossed. They were going to war
on the other side. To fight for the stranger's right to know,

for the models in the picture that comes with the frame,
and all others who seek freedom from liberty
and movies about movies about movies.

"The room in the mirror is full of carbon monoxide.
That's why we cannot pass without these chrome suits.

If the other side looks identical, study closely,
you'll see an object that's not in the room
you're standing in. Like a lute on the dresser,
partially hidden by compacts and atomizers."

The Mirrornauts vanished into the glass.

We are living in unwritten Bible stories, he thought.

That God created forest clearings
so he could spy on the Indians.

CXVII.

Deep within the interior of a Polish joke
where time slowly reduces the stairs into ramps

and men with hospital haircuts sit in focus groups
discussing the algebra of back pain

and the "Power of Not Caring."
Here in some mother-in-law's version of Poland
where even the magicians are regulated by the state.

He walked to the window and said
"Night, you fucking challenger, here I am."

Through the mirror he heard the war cry
of the $C_8H_{17}NO_4S$ Indians.

His back hurt.

CXXVI.

From our upstairs porch I watch my neighbor, a smalltown
accountant with a voice like a toy keyboard, begin his walk to work in
a navy blue Botany 500 suit, bought used in an L.A. consignment store
while visiting his widower son-in-law and blind grandaughter, and
according to my neighbor, formerly owned by Gene Rayburn, the
retired game show host whose grotesque aura still haunts the seven
o'clock time slots of my body's internal clock along with Merv Griffin,
Don Rickles, Cloris Leachman, Bert Convy, Wink Martindale and
the tenants of every Hollywood square; those horrible hucksters, sick-
ening adults/hyenas who seem to have had their protégés on every
Main Street, the men with perms, tight gray curls erupting over the
alcoholic topography of their oiled faces, a legion of salesmen ruined
by bad translations of an already disastrous California ideal, their eyes
stinking like boiled cocktail onions as they emerged from "sleek"
1980 Thunderbirds, all marinated teeth and snowplow mustaches,
fresh from invigorating divorces, dragging tawny S-shaped girlfriends
by the wrist to wooden gargoyle waterbeds where stereo systems
built into the headboards played "Eye in the Sky" by the Alan Parsons
Project endlessly through the night.

These men quietly disappeared sometime during the first Reagan
Administration. If the Mirrornauts did come for them, then they
must have leapt down through the bedroom ceilings, and the men
must have woken up screaming as their carpeting was ripped up, the
aquariums smashed with baseball bats, and then angry, insane, "my
ex-wife is behind this isn't she," obscure cuss words, now lost to us,
spilling out of their fat mouths.

CXXXII.

Inside an abandoned spa
where Swiss hardcore kids squat in polar rooms
underneath fountains of careless feedback,

or within the funeral home's fusebox
which operates the violet shadows on the lawn
and the digital eyes of an elk head
bolted above the respirating fireplace,

you, on the edge of rainshot shadows,

con the world into lamenting anything
until no one can recall how true stories end.

If it existed, we'd be used to it already,
the dream of important mail
like trumpets crashing into men
or oceans cruising through the furious night
while lonely seaside dentists hasten
to incorporate chocolate towers
into their huge immovable desserts.

If we are lured into violent matinees
we are only acting as the agents of coin circulation.
Like stuffed animals sharing coffee in the dorms,
or interstate median castaways with wild children,

we are all auditioning for a newish testament
where perfect kids ride pedestals of surf onto the beach
and Lake Speed's legendary hair rots
west of the redrock balconies and neutral horses

with fiery games.

CXVI.

A man walked into a bar at sunset, took his hat off and wiped his brow
with the back of his shirtsleeve.
"After a hard day's work you deserve a cold beer," said the bartender.
"Gimme a cold beer," he said. "It's been a long day but its all worth
it now."
The rest of the work crew walked into the bar.
"We've been working hard and now working time is through,"
they said.
"There's nothing like a cold beer when all is said and done."
"Man this beer hits the spot," said one, "all day long, while I was
working, I was imagining how good this was gonna taste."
"Yeah, there's nothing like an ice cold beer after a hard day's work,"
said another.

CLI.

A mutt barks at the service entrance
as the foursome, still using their bridge game aliases,
climb up to the bedrooms.

A computer would jam under all the distractions
in a watchdog's eye or, scrolling through a long list
of contemporary enemies (headed by "shape-shifters"),
never recognize the Smokers as they scale
the award-winning garden walls.

North goes down on East and the branches out the window
shift like scars on a toymaker's hand.

When he's finished he gets up and walks to the bathroom
where a Smoker is waiting and beats him until
his body is rich with contusions.

"Getting hurt makes a doctor a better doctor" he mutters and climbs out the open window.

New York, New York

A second New York is being built
a little west of the old one.
Why another, no one asks,
just build it, and they do.

The city is still closed off
to all but the work crews
who claim it's a perfect mirror image.

Truthfully, each man works on the replica
of the apartment building he lives in,
adding new touches,
like cologne dispensers, rock gardens,
and doorknobs marked for the grand hotels.

Improvements here and there, done secretly
and off the books. None of the supervisors
notice or mind. Everyone's in a wonderful mood,
joking, taking walks through the still streets
that the single reporter allowed inside has described as

"unleavened with reminders of the old city's complicated past,
but giving off some blue perfume from the early years on earth."

The men grow to love the peaceful town.
It becomes more difficult to return home at night,

which sets the wives to worrying.
The yellow soups are cold, the sunsets quick.

The men take long breaks on the fire escapes,
waving across the quiet spaces to other workers
meditating on their perches.

Until one day...

The sky fills with charred clouds.
Toolbelts rattle in the rising wind.

Something is wrong.

A foreman stands in the avenue
pointing binoculars at a massive gray mark
moving towards us in the eastern sky.

Several voices, What, What is it?

Pigeons, he yells through the wind.

The Night Nurse Essays

When he started the Night Nurse Essays
the idea was to patch together a book
that described itself over and over again,
comprised of thousands of black chains
that were dragged through green rocks and river stairs
to arrive haunted, unscheduled and lit from above.

There were long days of bad ideas
when he felt his book was ineffective
like a watercolor of a fire engine
or a statue of the fastest man alive,

and he would go to the window
and watch the fireflies
criss cross without insight,
then turning around
sometimes notice his wife Asterisk
lifting dinner to the table.

One night, up considering dead realms,
he heard the sustained woof of a dog.
It drew him up and propelled him outside
to walk cowed under the fierce starlight.

He crossed against the light
at the corner of Night School and Fake Badge
concentrating so hard on certain experimental
passages of the Declaration of Independence
that he did not notice

the woman rising up from behind a mailbox
wearing a necklace strung with diary keys.
"Help me, you f*@#," she whispered,
"I'm losing my reflection."

She dragged a lame foot behind her
into the Onyx Lounge.
He stood and watched the night
push itself into the bar
and the light push it back out.

He couldn't go back home to sleep,
not back to his unorganized dreams,
always set on the concourses of dead airports.
(His essays filling the seat pockets of empty jets.)

That was when he decided to walk down
to Jewish Name Lake, to sit by the shore
and wait for the sunrise.

That's where they found the body.

Many weeks have passed now,
the lottery jackpot has grown unbelievably large,
and still we have no idea
how he came to die in that lake.

Perhaps he could not bear to think
of his name only surviving in the index
of someone else's biography.

Or he was recalled by a higher power, having—
I don't know—masturbated too many times
in a drugstore Halloween mask.

Maybe he was assassinated by an obscure resistance group.
His essays on menopause in the Amish community
and the anthropology of the smalltown drug deal
had ruffled a few feathers.

In that case his final words may have been damaged,
dormant expressions clambering out of their graves
with dust on the unstressed syllables,

before he was rudely shoved into the lake.

Pulled down through the cool green chambers,
we like to imagine him struggling awake
and suddenly realizing
he was seeing rain
in its original uncut form.

From Guide to the Graves of British Actors

If you have loved the light
    of guest rooms in the morning,

and built plot and theme
    and finally setting sun

onto the flat earth of chessboards,

then to die on contemporary furniture

with John Webster's antique jive on your lips,

after a long life lived in that pause

where a guest studies his ice cubes

    and listens to the room tick,

would rinse the larger stillness with whole moments
    lost in yawns.

Even if you have never been served by a butler

and even if movies have prepared you
    on how to react to his attentions,

when it finally comes to pass,

sitting in an armchair
    beneath a tangle of nicotine swans,

you are completely aware of your role as the American Guest

and surprised at how he, the butler,
                               faintly smells of silver polish,

and the English snow,
how it glitters down on our wide emergency

without reference to the fact of it happening.

Serenade for a Wealthy Widow

Nude descending staircase headless,
not knowing where she is going
but brave because all dreams lack conclusions
and she is not enlisted to an ending.

The abstract cannons in the background
are still unfired, still the temperature of a bird,
while a depth charge buried in blue paint
speckles the door plaques and crab apples of S Street.

In the morning you rise from your bed
and the self-portraits come streaming in.
A cold black maple hanger clatters to the floor
sputtering police language now, blank, now.

Ideas reach out with dwarf arms, rheumy-eyed,
covered in weak syntax and powderburns.

From here at your office near the end of the river
where messages still trickle in from the interior

like *I am here* and *I am still here.*

The Homeowner's Prayer

The moment held two facets in his mind.
The sound of lawns cut late in the evening
and the memory of a push-up regimen he had abandoned.

It was Halloween.

An alumni newsletter lay on the hall table
but he would not/could not read it,
for his hands were the same emotional structures
in 1987 as they had been in 1942.

Nothing had changed. He had retained his tendency
to fall in love with supporting actresses
renowned for their near miss with beauty

and coffee still caused the toy ideas
he used to try out on the morning carpools,
a sweeping reorganization of the company softball league,
or how to remove algae from the windows of a houseboat.

He remembered a morning when the carpool
had been discussing how they'd like to die.
The best way to go.

He said, why are you talking about this.
Just because everyone has died so far,
doesn't mean that we're going to die.

But he had waited too long to speak.
They were already in the parking garage.

And now two of them had passed away.

It was Halloween.

Another Pennsylvania sunset
backed down the local mountain

spraying the colors of a streetfighter's face
onto the narrative wallpaper of a boy's bedroom.

Once he thought all he would ever need
was a house with time and circumstance.

He slowly made his way into the kitchen
and filled a bowl with apples and raisins.

The clock was learning to be 6:34.

The willows bent to within decimals of the lawn.

It was Halloween.

From His Bed in the Capital City

The Highway Commissioner dreams of us.
We are driving by Christmas tree farms
wearing wedding rings with on/off switches,
composing essays on leg room in our heads.

We know there is policy like ice sculpture,
policy that invisibly dictates the shape
of the freeway forests and the design
of the tollbooths that passing children
send their minds into.

Photography's remainder is sound and momentum,
which we were looking to pare off the edges
of the past anyway, so snapshots of Mom
with a kitchen table hill of cocaine
or the dog frozen in the attitude
of eating raw hamburger
get filed under "Misc. Americana,"
though only partially contained there,
as beads of sap are always leaking
from the columns of the bar graph.

The voices of the bumperstickers tangle in our heads
like cafeteria noise and we can't help but be aware
that by making this trip, by driving home for Christmas,
we are assuming some classic role.
It is the role he has cast us in: "holiday travelers."

He dreams us safely into our driveways
and leaves us at the flickering doors.

Nervous Ashers

There were mountain huts full of smallpox strung out along the hillsides between Escatawpa and Morgan City, birds boiling up and out of freestanding chimneys under the routine advent of rainbows and chainsaws, the old sound of cheap labor rising and falling in the weather that was like frosted bank glass and advancing. There were heaps of tangled sawhorses and tripwire, vacant jasper and wolframite mines, mounds of dead Ataris and scarred desk drawer Bibles scattered across those abandoned counties that lay inert as rope.

Hazel and Bobby lived together in an old slave shack I rented out in the upper fields. They cut Canadian thistle and picked sloe berries off the blackthorn for a living, slashing their hands and bickering all day in the frayed heat, visiting me in the cool mainhouse most evenings. We'd sit in the rooms without ceilings, drinking white hill whiskey under the recombinant stars, and Bobby, who loved to go on about things, would reminisce about his dead wife who'd contracted a disease from sleeping too close to the boxfan. On Sundays they wouldn't move a muscle. They'd just sit there like two piles of coins, quietly warming through the afternoon, then slowly cooling off over the evening.

Bobby puts on his sound jacket. Shards of hospital bed are locked in the bass drum. Through the worn dolichoid rafters I can see birds flying over the practice room. The snare is stuffed with traffic tickets and out the window there's my horse walking on the stream, the stream always behind schedule. There's a dust mote hawk landing in slo-mo on my guitar. Hazel's saying something about Earnest Wourlds over in Tullahoma who'd had a dream about a cougar sleepwalking on Polk's grave and how that was bad luck for the region. ("Those that look out the window are darkened. All those faces passed down through the centuries that kickstart the rivers and grow like nerve endings in a coal cart until they're key-cold and shoved through the deathgate, a catafalque set free, released into the dirtways.") "And John and his father John trap mink under the chain lightning in the libraries they've landed in, where all the talk about shadow-dappled paths is typeset, published and poured into a break in the earth," Hazel murmured to no one in the room. You might think it was all words and dark tickets as we began to play "R.M.T" in the swarming weather chart sundown, and it was.

Outside you'd still hear the music, hear someone singing "actors dreaming got nowhere to stay/see my sheet go walking run and fly," and it would sound better from far away, like a faded sketch of a long forgotten pacer at the Downs, all the while platinum ticks are dropping off the trees like little Romans, onto an auburn shower-curtain half-buried in the forest floor.

Already gone were the golden days of e-z credit, the days of approaching squat south-central skylines from underneath the ice blue tides of the windshield, the five cent war comets, howling saran yaps and careening school chords. All that was left, looking like two lost eyeballs on the field after Spotsylvania, were a couple of black plastic knobs in the dirt, one for tone and one for rinse.

This place is like a haunted turnpike, closed down for years, where things still happen in the little turnoffs to the renowned teenagers that never came back.

If you come in the day and you're lucky, you might catch yourself a nice photograph of two sweatbees fucking on a coke mirror. You might see my horse breaking across a white wine-colored clearing, or maybe hear the old chords coming, for no real reason, out of sockets in the walls. ("because there's an answering machine clogged with ice, deep in the Courthouse Mountains where he lived and died in the breach.")

April 13, 1865

At first the sound had no meaning.
The shot came from the balcony,
as if the play had sprung an annex,
and I, John Sleeper Clarke,
pictured stars through oak scaffolds
as the news traveled over
the chairscape like a stain.

In that dark room lit by gas jets
the Welshman to my left conceded
the armrest we'd been fighting over
and doctors and half doctors
flowed into the scarlet aisles
to help.

I did not take to the image
of a bay mare waiting in the alley
or a manhunt through Maryland.

I remember standing up
as the others did,

and how the assassin was in mid-air
when the stagehands wheeled out clouds.

Self-Portrait at 28

I know it's a bad title
but I'm giving it to myself as a gift
on a day nearly canceled by sunlight
when the entire hill is approaching
the ideal of Virginia
brochured with goldenrod and loblolly
and I think "at least I have not woken up
with a bloody knife in my hand"
by then having absently wandered
one hundred yards from the house
while still seated in this chair
with my eyes closed.

It is a certain hill.
The one I imagine when I hear the word "hill,"
and if the apocalypse turns out
to be a world-wide nervous breakdown,
if our five billion minds collapse at once,
well I'd call that a surprise ending
and this hill would still be beautiful,
a place I wouldn't mind dying
alone or with you.

I am trying to get at something
and I want to talk very plainly to you
so that we are both comforted by the honesty.

You see, there is a window by my desk
I stare out when I'm stuck,
though the outdoors has rarely inspired me to write
and I don't know why I keep staring at it.

My childhood hasn't made good material either,
mostly being a mulch of white minutes

with a few stand out moments:
popping tar bubbles on the driveway in the summer,
a certain amount of pride at school
everytime they called it "our sun,"
and playing football when the only play
was "go out long" are what stand out now.

If squeezed for more information
I can remember old clock radios
with flipping metal numbers
and an entree called Surf and Turf.

As a way of getting in touch with my origins,
every night I set the alarm clock
for the time I was born, so that waking up
becomes a historical reenactment

and the first thing I do
is take a reading of the day
and try to flow with it,
like when you're riding a mechanical bull
and you strain to learn the pattern quickly
so you don't inadvertently resist it.

II.

I can't remember being born
and no one else can remember it either
even the doctor who I met years later
at a cocktail party.

It's one of the little disappointments
that makes you think about getting away,
going to Holly Springs or Coral Gables

and taking a room on the square
with a landlady whose hands are scored
by disinfectant, telling the people you meet
that you are from Alaska, and listen
to what they have to say about Alaska
until you have learned much more about Alaska
than you ever will about Holly Springs or Coral Gables.

Sometimes I'm buying a newspaper
in a strange city and think
"I am about to learn what it's like to live here."
Oftentimes there's a news item
about the complaints of homeowners
who live beside the airport
and I realize that I read an article
on this subject nearly once a year
and always receive the same image:

I am in bed late at night
in my house near the airport
listening to the jets fly overhead,
a strange wife sleeping beside me.
In my mind the bedroom is an amalgamation
of various cold medicine commercial sets
(there is always a box of tissue on the nightstand).

I know these recurring news articles are clues,
flaws in the design, though I haven't figured out
how to string them together yet.
But I'm noticing that the same people
are dying over and over again,

for instance, Minnie Pearl
who died this year
for the fourth time in four years.

III.

Today is the first day of Lent
and once again I'm not really sure what it is.
How many more years will I let pass
before I take the trouble to ask someone?

It reminds me of this morning
when you were getting ready for work.
I was sitting by the space heater,
numbly watching you dress,
and when you asked why I never wear a robe
I had so many good reasons
I didn't know where to begin.

If you were cool in high school
you didn't ask too many questions.
You could tell who'd been to last night's
big metal concert by the new t-shirts in the hallways.
You didn't have to ask
and that's what cool was:
the ability to deduce,
to know without asking.
And the pressure to simulate coolness
means not asking when you don't know,
which is why kids grow ever more stupid.

A yearbook's endpages, filled with promises
to stay in touch, stand as proof of the uselessness
of a teenager's promise. Not like I'm dying
for a letter from the class stoner
ten years on but...

Do you remember the way the girls
would call out "love you!"
conveniently leaving out the "I"

as if they didn't want to commit
to their own declaration.

I agree that the "I" is a pretty heavy concept
and hope you won't get uncomfortable
if I should go into some deeper stuff here.

IV.

There are things I've given up on
like recording funny answering-machine messages.
It's part of growing older
and the human race as a group
has matured along the same lines.
It seems our comedy dates the quickest.
If you laugh out loud at Shakespeare's jokes
I hope you won't be insulted
if I say you're trying too hard.
Even sketches from the original Saturday Night Live
seem slow-witted and obvious now.

It's just that our advances are irrepressible.
Nowadays little kids can't even set up lemonade stands.
It makes people too self-conscious about the past,
though try explaining that to a kid.

I'm not saying it should be this way.

All this new technology
will eventually give us new feelings
that will never completely displace the old ones,
leaving everyone feeling quite nervous
and split in two.

We will travel to Mars
even as folks on Earth
are still ripping open potato chip
bags with their teeth.

Why? I don't have the time or intelligence
to make all the connections,
like my friend Gordon
(this is a true story)
who, having grown up in Braintree, Massachusetts,
had never pictured a brain snagged in a tree
until I brought it up.
He'd never broken the name down to its parts.
By then it was too late.
He had moved to Coral Gables.

V.

The hill out my window is still looking beautiful,
suffused in a kind of gold national park light,
and it seems to say,
I'm sorry the world could not possibly
use another poem about Orpheus
but I'm available if you're not working
on a self-portrait or anything.

I'm watching my dog have nightmares,
twitching and whining on the office floor,
and I try to imagine what beast
has cornered him in the meadow
where his dreams are set.

I'm just letting the day be what it is:
a place for a large number of things

to gather and interact—
not even a place but an occasion,
a reality for real things.

Friends warned me not to get too psychedelic
or religious with this piece:
"they won't accept it if it's too psychedelic
or religious," but these are valid topics
and I'm the one with the dog twitching on the floor,
possibly dreaming of me,
that part of me that would beat a dog
for no good reason,
no reason that a dog could see.

I am trying to get at something so simple
that I have to talk plainly
so the words don't disfigure it,
and if it turns out that what I say is untrue,
then at least let it be harmless
like a leaky boat in the reeds
that is bothering no one.

VI.

I can't trust the accuracy of my own memories,
many of them having blended with sentimental
telephone and margarine commercials,
plainly ruined by Madison Avenue,
though no one seems to call the advertising world
"Madison Avenue" anymore. Have they moved?
I need an update on this.

But first I have some business to take care of.

I walked out to the hill behind our house
which looks positively Alaskan today,
and it would be easier to explain this
if I had a picture to show you,
but I was with our young dog
and he was running through the tall grass
like running through the tall grass
is all of life together,
until a bird calls or he finds a beer can
and that thing fills all the space in his head.

You see,
his mind can only hold one thought at a time
and when he finally hears me call his name
he looks up and cocks his head.
For a single moment
my voice is everything:

Self-portrait at 28.

3.

From Cantos for James Michener: Part I

XXV.

I left my appendix in a North African motel.

An organ lost to time like hatchecks
and the Scottish word for "war."

We were braiding birdsongs into white noise,

asleep in our horse-drawn beds

(And it feels good to get arrested

To sleep in thickets of wild aspirin

with the Duchess of Night Soccer)

when dice rolled out of his hand
like paratroopers out of a thundercloud.

The evening train is a literary device.

God surfaces in a crossword puzzle.

Momma died at the Food Lion.

XLII.

After the robbery we found a pentagram carefully laid out
in electrical tape on the kitchen floor.

Someone had jerked off over an open phone book
imagining municipal orgies

on the gray landscape of a calculator's window.

He mentioned something about the "infant baker"—
some kind of prescience or entity from Chicago.

Still disturbed by the size of softballs

Just back from my People Against Love meeting

I picked up some champagne, a rent-a-car, astroturf wildflowers

and a copy of Charles Lamb's "Satan In Search of a Wife,
by an Eyewitness."

For my kindergarten teacher whose breasts
cast shadows on the innocents.

XLIII.

Many of the men who kissed her later died
in so-called "industrial accidents."

God will know them by their fingerprints,

battery diagrams carved faintly into the black plastic,

Couplets sealed with Judaic frost,

In my lost long ago.

LXVIII.

At night in Keswick, I listen to the refrains of the state road.

The results of an eye exam on the coffee table.

I have gone underground with the apologists for cocaine

who stand in the bus shelter like a Wall Street crèche.

We were like two teams fighting without mascots,

A lesbian storing her zygotes in an old Zenith TV

As the band broke into "Symphony Usher Blues"

On a Monday morning when the universe felt finished.

LXXII.

So dull that he only makes a brief appearance
in his own life story,

resurfacing in a Florida legend, he kills himself
on a beautiful day.

In the avant-garde hospital (let me explain what I mean by that)

Where blue deer speak Fortran in the restroom,

I remember going to the post office and seeing my masseur's
face on the most wanted list,
remember leaving New York after a party
where a choreographer tried to convince me
that bluejeans were "pretentious

nineteenth-century gold rush period" outfits,

that the ancient world was a stage for the superstars of the Bible.

It was final then. The "wheel" would be his great metaphor.

The Declaration of Independence blew me away when I first read it.

To the days beyond this one which are still perfect.

Come on.

CORAL GABLES

She wore a dress of voting booth curtains
to a party at the coroner's split-level ranch.
As she dashed up the quartz pebble lane
a bell pushed by the wind rang.

Her initial entrance was unrecorded.
Under the wagon wheel chandelier
a Bible story shot back through her mind
whirling and open to the page:
"You will meet a stranger."

A man worked on his wife in the foyer,
"That agent had you over a barrel.
He kept his car running in the driveway
and you rushed out to it."

Inching along the wall
she stared at the storms in the wood's grain

until a nervous young man leaned over and whispered

"I hired a detective to investigate myself.
It was an act of religious passion.
He's probably here at this party—watching me."

She stepped backwards, over a dog jackknifed on the rug
and fell into the arms of a scholar who spoke of an ad
he'd discovered running unanswered for one hundred years,

floating like a ghostship over the classifieds.

The coroner's walls were decorated with magic-
marker drawings of wicker chairs and race cars.

The notebook paper trembled when the heat came on.

No one drinks rye anymore, someone said.
No one feels that way anymore.

She left the party at midnight, on the arm of a man
who had carved a government agency's initials
into a tree as a teenager.

"I refuse to be the middleman in a relationship
between you and the florist."

As they walked through the city,
he explained why he would never buy her flowers.

The New Idea

From a third floor window I spray a sad look
down into the courtyard of the office park
filled with cold pebbles and benches.

There are little donuts for sale in the breakroom
vending machine called gems or donettes

or gemettes, I can't remember,
and I'd rather not retrace the string of decisions

that have left me stupefied before an inspirational
poster that claims "The First Word In *Can't* Is *Can.*"

Due to its dense history of uncomfortable moments,
our elevator is haunted with poorly conceived smiles
and sinking hearts, so I take the stairs

to the boardroom and pass a mailroom clerk
with reggae leaking out his walkman

and a crumpled secretary who,
as the cruel office rumor goes,

keeps a thermos on her desk filled
with the ashes of her dead bulldog.

It would be difficult to admit that no one
ushered me as a blip onto this cold grid,

no one asked me to design my life
to fit the dimensions of this situation,

stranded in an office whose walls
are strange mathematical mountains,

so out of touch with my own body

that I watch my handwriting appear on a legal pad
like rainspots on a sidewalk.

I was in high school
when I realized that not doing anything

was categorically different from deciding to do nothing,
but beauty blew a fuse, the hold music put me in a trance,

and what was black and heading towards me
transported me here like a cow in a comic hurricane.

Our CEO is in Asia and the staff has gathered
in the boardroom for his televised conference call.

An inter-office newsletter is passed around
by a clerk I once caught pressing warm xerox copies

to his face and who later tried to shake my hand
in the men's room. "The universe, she is a bitch,"

he said, and I liked him for not knowing that men
characteristically shut down in restrooms.

I suppose it's difficult to work with people
who are comfortable inside of nightmares,

though even the numbest of us are intimidated
by the unnatural bulk of "his" life story

by "his" portrait hanging on the east wall,
glowing with rush hour romance, hair groomed

into place by the soft breezes of annuity,
in this room where many times I have seen the world

end in a vice-president's inadvertent comment and
suddenly start up again with a slight retraction.

I shake a few hands,
never precisely sure when to let go,

and the monitor flickers on, revealing the Chairman

wearing a white robe, sleeping in a Chinese stream
with a single chrysanthemum tucked behind his ear.

His arms are like slackened chain
in the puttering current.

Our pens hover over the legal pads.
We are to understand something by this,

a Providence engineered to go void at five,
glassed over by the fantastic qualities of gin,

cast as we are into this underimagined place.

How I Met Your Mother

"You can tell he has an older brother," she said.
"How," I wondered, "do you know that."
"By the BB scars on his ass."

We watched "motherfuckers" crackle out of his mouth.
He wanted something. Something like a mini-mart blowjob.
She popped open her briefcase and pulled out
a stack of research on tonight's guests.

I was surprised she was willing to share information.
We'd been rivals for eight years, writing the society pages
for our town's two daily newspapers.

Truth told, I wasn't up on this crowd.
I'd only heard rumors about the house on Route 727
where they used a nineteen letter alphabet
and held nude parties fueled by five dollar bills
pulled out of birthday cards by the host,
a postal clerk with a sharp eye for grandmotherly script.

"OK," I said, "who is Mr. Wide World of Whiskey by the bean dip?"
She glanced down at her notes. "He just opened a salon
by the courthouse for defendants who want the innocent look."

The subject was listening to a woman bitch about parrots.
"They talk but they don't understand!"
"If animals could really talk, we would have killed them
off years ago," he said dryly.

"How about the lady in the orange crossing-guard sash?"

"Part of the downtown crowd.
She paints portraits of children who cut in line."

I recognized the fellow she was talking to.
A Spanish exchange student. His lust
had scorched several area trellises.

A very old man came out of the guest room
and walked up to them.

His necktie acted as a valve
that kept the sadness bottled in.

"Federico, I'd like you to meet Elmer of Elmer's Glue."

My exact thought was, "no way…"
I faked a disinterested look around the room.
On the wall behind me hung a framed photograph,
"nephew with first stereo,"
and a painting called "Three Ideas About Maine."

The old man approached us, pulling an oxygen tank
on a little chrome cart. He wore a checked sportscoat
covered in industry medals that clattered when he moved.

It was taking him forever to reach us.

I guess we both looked at the phone and thought about
calling the story in for the morning edition,

but there was something more finely drawn in the air
than the dotted line that showed our possible paths to the phone.

She took my writing hand in hers,
and after that I could find no precedent.

They Don't Acknowledge the Letter C

He thought back to the time
he had blown his son's mind
by making him count stars.
    "And don't come in until you're finished."

It wasn't what he had intended, he said
as the kitchen clock twitched,
    still wired to the universe's anatomy.

He was my assistant wrestling coach,
sobbing in the white ruins of his kitchen
for the olde tymes when the towne hospital was fringed
    with icicles
    and the dogtrack
stands were packed with his friends.

Instead of helping I sat and watched,
desperately afraid that someone would append
    a suffix to my name.

It was the marks on my chest,
(bruises from the porn magazines I propped there)
that started the rumors about auxiliary
    alphabets in my home.

"There are more bears in one N.H. county," I recited at school,
"than in all of Europe."

That was long before I discovered the zen of hospitalization

in the archipelago of living rooms that became
    the center of my physical world,

wandering through medieval Wyomings
as a figure in the distance even to my own eye.

For a long time I dreamed of moving
    to the outskirts of town
where you can still burn trash
and see the stars glitter like errors in the sky.

There is a porch where we drink on deck chairs
and when we drink we imagine the oceans receding,

the dark beaches sloping down like cinema floors.

A yard dog that has grown into the color of his food
watches a set of birds move through the ring of blue darkness
above Richmond,

the rain comes down at a slant
    as if shot by Indians

and we are not even close to being through.

Democratic Vistas

The narrator was shot by the sniper he was describing
and I quickly picked up his pen.

What luck, I thought, to be sitting up here in the narrator's
tower where the parking lots look like chalkboards and the characters
scurry around or fall down and die as I design it.

Then I started to read the novel I'd inherited, and didn't like
what I discovered.

Most of the characters were relentlessly evil, taken right off the bad
streets of the Bible.

The narrator would interrupt the story at all the wrong times, like a
third wheel on a date, and deliver shaky opinions like "People who
wear turtlenecks must have really fucked-up necks."

He would get lost in pointless investigations, i.e., was Pac-Man an
animal, so that when we returned to the characters many pages
later, their hair had grown past the shoulder and their fingernails
were inches long.

In support of the novel, I must say it was designed well. The scenes
were like rowhouses. They had common sidewalls, through which one
could hear the faint voices and footsteps of what was to come.

I've lived those long driving scenes. Everyone knows how hard it is,
after you've been on the road all day, to stop driving. You go to sleep
and the road runs under the bed like a filmstrip.

I also liked the sheriff's anxious dream sequence, where he keeps
putting a two-inch-high man in jail, and the tiny man keeps walking
out, in between the bars.

After a sleepless night he's awoken by the phone. There's a sniper in the University tower. The sheriff stands before the bathroom mirror. Drops of Visine are careening down his face.

They are cold and clear
and I can count them through my rifle scope.

Piano and Scene

A child needs to know the point of the holiday.

His aunt is saying grace over a decaffeinated coffee
and her daughter is reading a Russian novel
whose 45 chapters are set
on 45 consecutive Valentine's Days.

Grandpa is telling the kids fairy tales
from Pennsylvania's pretzel-making region

and it's hard for me to be in the mood
you need me to be in right now,

as I'm suddenly wrapped up in this speculation
on the as yet undiscovered moods of the future,

like nostalgia for a discontinued model of robot
or patriotic feelings for your galaxy

which will probably resemble nostalgia and patriotism
as we now know it, but with added tiers of complexity.

Even if we could manage to travel in time, who's to say
we could relate with those who receive us?

Perhaps we would not be able to read the expressions
on our own descendants faces for what they mean.

As advanced as we consider ourselves,
we still allow ad copy to pander to us.
The scam exposed, it endures with our permission
as a parallel narrative running beside our lives
where we sit with an unbuttered baked potato
and a warm beer in multiple versions of Akron
leavened with foreclosure, heartburn and rain.

Great-grandfather's hobbies, whether they be botany or magic,
can barely make sense to a boy named Occupant III.

Their genius was to let us criticize them
until it became boring and obvious to do so.

Meanwhile they were up ahead, busily constructing a world
in which boring and obvious criticism
was about the worst thing you could do,
and when we reached them in time they were waiting
with their multiple Akrons,
always one link ahead in the chain of consent.

Maybe we need to give up on these simplistic
"us vs. them" oppositions that we shouldn't believe in,
but in our anger do.

Perhaps we should be concentrating
on what's going to happen an hour or two from now,

whether the human race will survive into this afternoon,
what kinds of food they will eat at the dinner table

and what tales they'll tell of this morning.

Of Things Found Where They Are Not Supposed To Be

I am shivering, reading cold northeastern prose
and there is a word for what I do
        but I do it anyway,
carefully setting dinner on the table uncooked,
        before setting the table on fire.

The sky hovers overhead holding up dotted lines drawn from
        the binoculars to the birds.

A woman whispers to her sugar bowl,
"Slowly, over time, you will be lent to the neighbors."

At the bus terminal, behind the candy machine,
there is a tunnel that comes out in the prison library,

and it's all pinned to a shimmering screen
        by the slide projector's cone of lit dust.

Can I safely say that Greece was mainly
        water, rock, and ideas?

My statistics show that several thousand years of rain
have done little damage to the planet,
yet imagine if that amount had fallen indoors.

Imagine this girl, a winsome beauty previously existing
only on a rejected coin design, imagine her driving through the old
seaboard slave states,
with a treasury of college fight songs,
        "in the tape deck."

The rose bushes look like Latin homework
        on the pond's reflective skin.

Like a "hullo!" up a rainpipe, it bears me homeward,

not asking for a quick peek at the shade inside objects,

but simply admiring the Precambrian skyline of the car keys
that took us away from the colony of motels
scattered like mushrooms about the beltway's exit ramp.

And yet it's so strange that we've come to this,
and to think that someday we'll come back to it
from the opposite direction.

On the streets I look out for people from the future.
They try to play it cool so no one notices, taking taxis,
calling the driver "Mac," in what they mistakenly
believe to be the lingo of the day.

When I see L.A. fireplaces reflected in L.A. wineglasses,
crows wired to the sky like marred pixels,
and "you" with your little tail of vowels,
I start to believe that the inscription above the portal
describes this side, not the next.

For now just keep smiling and nodding
as if you were in a foreign country,
painfully grasping a pineapple.

A Letter from Isaac Asimov to His Wife Janet, Written On His Deathbed

One night, studying an egg tray in my kitchen, that first novel fell together in my mind: apes blowing blood into the air, the robot nymphs dipping their slender metal legs into an ammonia brook.

I began those flights from Earth in plywood space capsules, fleeing to a place Satan could not find. That was my hope. Getting away from the chain letters, fever, rats, and unemployment, away from the dark uncles that strayed over the globe, cutting brake lines and loosening screws.

And as a Jew I asked myself what good are hidden things, and as a Jew I admonished myself for asking. I knew that the best things were hidden, and all of this was said in a private voice, a cousin to the one I used to speak to pets.

I am writing this under the illumination of an old American stereo. For once I don't want to know the weather forecast. In fact, I can't bear to hear it. The jealousy would kill me before midnight. Perhaps they will make jokes at Doubleday tomorrow.
I can imagine an intern asking, "What were his last ten thousand words..."

I want to know too. From my sickbed I've seen cellophane rams shimmering in the yard and cardinals that look like quarts of blood balanced in the branches. The doctor calls them apparitions. Perhaps my last words will be random.

I am so drowsy, here listening to the wild dressage of a housefly, thinking about the loyal robots in my paperbacks. Thinking about the little chalet I would have built for you on Neptune.

A Neptune indiscernible from Vermont.

Virginia Mines: The Mascara Series

We took rooms
in the roomless village

on a little afternoon
when the world was smoke.

The frayed fountains
(it was autumn in the slums)

sang the pop and country charts,
a checked-out treasury of hearsay

and Dutch plays about air
on bridges without chasms.

O the beautiful sayings!

It was a record hot day
with the anti-banking kids,

their crazy Jamestown energy
draining into the grave

of Miss Universe 1797.

We had inaugural day whitecaps
and fifth floor birds,

a supreme court electrician
by the Wonderful Town Sea,

it was twilight
in the winston ultra lights era

when Pa wrote the report
on the North American

upholstered trap door
and "The World as Bad Idea."

The playing cards had tricked themselves
into a bad life as toys,

and we hit the road
in a walking contraption.

We passed the mortgaged colonials
in the year the trees reached the attic.

We saw "Moon over Woolite Bottle"
and the grand robot portraits

trembling like second animals
with the energy in a painter's arm,

distributing what we half knew
in multiple western towns,

where we learned how to be free,
how to get out,

that fixity was a famous dream
and today a variation on yesterday.
Still, a rational brat
with a red foam mustache

could dial "I" for Intellectual
and get oak ontologies

late in the afternoon
if he had a dead language and a dime.

The rainbow hardened into pentameter
and we found phones in the coal box

making the wilderness negative again.
It had a name that obscured its purpose,

"Poeme concerning renaissance faire."
Like a mousetrap it had one muscle,

and like sleep
it combined death and tourism.

We went days without noticing our bodies,
convinced the most important thing

we could give the world
was the truth of our lives.

Even your basic "I am alone,"
freezing in the shadow of a house.

We were strangers without suitcases
trying to make you remember us,
painting "black object with red splotch,"
ready to unload our ideas upon a kid

as if water was what we really wanted
when we asked for a glass of it,

confessing our devotion to resemblances
on the yellowed breakdance charts

that we studied by candlelight,
like toys caught reading

their own directions.

Now II

I am not in the parlor of a federal brownstone.
I am not a cub scout seduced by Iron Maiden's mirror worlds.

I'm on a floor unrecognized by the elevator,
    fucked beyond understanding
    like a hacked up police tree
on the outskirts of town.

Father, why does this night
last longer than any other night?

For God is not a secret.

And the brown girl who reads the Bible by the pool
with a bookmark that says "ed called"
or "ed call ed," must know that turtles
are screwed in the snow

and that everything strains to be inevitable
even as it's being killed forever.

And this is also a song.

O I've lied to you so much I can no longer trust you.
O Don't people wear out from the inside,

Why must we suffer this expensive silence,
aren't we meant to crest in a fury more distinguished?

Because there is my life and there is our life
    (which I know to be Your life).

Dear Lord, whom I love so much,
    I don't think I can change anymore.

I have burned all my forces at the edge of the city.
I am all dressed up to go away,

and I'm asking You now
    if You'd take me as I am.

For God is not a secret,

and this also is a song.

The War in Apartment 1812

Years had been lashed onto years,
and we existed behind the strange
front doors of New Jersey,
our suitcases warping beside the radiators
while every other object of perception waited
for our touch beneath an inch of paint.

There must be a painless way to remember
the way the apple trees tangled up,
and rain came down on the Gulf station,
or the pastures on the back of a nickel
like the decimals in our initials,
falling hard and clean upon everything.

There was a skull and a Christmas tree,
a flask of white hill whiskey
on the walnut secretary.
All things rigid in their arrangements,
        coiled up in autumn's marble,

and I couldn't trust them to remain.

The Double Bell of Heat

Midway down Walnut Street
a yellow sign says Slow Deaf Child,
with the silhouette of a running boy

painted over the bent and dented surface.
Just the post, rusted to black,
gives the story away.

The child must have grown up
and left the neighborhood a long time ago.

And now there's this sign.

You can imagine his parents going
to the city clerk's office.

The paperwork is strange and complex,
languishing in office out-bins,
drifting through council meetings.

One spring morning the boy sees two city workers
get out of a truck and set the bright sign
in the patch of grass between the sidewalk and street.

He watches it out the window, knowing what it is,
watching it gather the world around it
like a mountain in the Bible.

Cars heed the sign, many drivers scanning to the left
and right hoping to catch sight of the deaf boy playing.

Some drivers imagine hitting him and slow down even more.
They play out the scene, what they would say,
how their lives would change.

And the years pass, even for the little deaf boy.

He gets married, has kids.
Maybe moves to a village in New England
with stone walls and candle makers.

You can imagine him returning to the old neighborhood.
Driving down on a fall afternoon into the quiet center of things,
gently braking before this old streetsign.

He would do that, he would come back.
As if it had been written twice.

David Berman was born in Williamsburg, Virginia in 1967. He graduated from the Greenhill School in Addison, Texas, the University of Virginia, and the University of Massachusetts. His band, the Silver Jews, has released five albums, *The Natural Bridge*, *Starlite Walker*, *American Water*, *Bright Flight*, and *Tanglewood Numbers* on Drag City Records. He lives in Nashville, Tennessee.

Thank you:
Rob Bingham, Connie Lovatt, Charles Wright, Mrs. Eastus, Rick Berman, Mimi Berman, Shep and Anita Berman, Robert Tissot, Dixie Berman, Dara Wier, Alexandra Tager, Joanna Yas, Kathryn Frazier, Brett Ralph, Betsey Schmidt, Patrick Whalen, Roe Ethridge, Cassie Marrett, and Meyer Helfenstein.